I SHOW GOOD SPORTSMANSHIP

T0009842

BY CHARLOTTE TAYLOR

Gareth Stevens
PUBLISHING

Please visit our website, www.garethstevens.com. For a free color catalog of all our high-quality books, call toll free 1-800-542-2595 or fax 1-877-542-2596.

Cataloging-in-Publication Data
Names: Taylor, Charlotte.
Title: I show good sportsmanship / Charlotte Taylor.
Description: New York : Gareth Stevens Publishing, 2021. | Series: We've got character! | Includes glossary and index.
Identifiers: ISBN 9781538256183 (pbk.) | ISBN 9781538256206 (library bound) | ISBN 9781538256190 (6 pack)
Subjects: LCSH: Sportsmanship–Juvenile literature. | Conduct of life–Juvenile literature.
Classification: LCC GV706.3 T39 2021 | DDC 175–dc23

Published in 2021 by
Gareth Stevens Publishing
111 East 14th Street, Suite 349
New York, NY 10003

Designer: Sarah Liddell
Editor: Megan Quick

Photo credits: Cover, pp. 1, 7 Monkey Business Images/Shutterstock.com; background throughout Igor Vitkovskiy/Shutterstock.com; p. 5 George Doyle/Stockbyte/Getty Images; p. 9 imagedb.com/Shutterstock.com; p. 11 Brocreative/Shutterstock.com; p. 13 Yuriy Golub/Shutterstock.com; p. 15 stockfour/Shutterstock.com; pp. 17, 19 SDI Productions/E+/Getty Images; p. 21 Suzanne Tucker/Shutterstock.com.

Printed in the United States of America

Some of the images in this book illustrate individuals who are models. The depictions do not imply actual situations or events.

CPSIA compliance information: Batch #CS20GS: For further information contact Gareth Stevens, New York, New York at 1-800-542-2595.

Find us on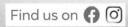

CONTENTS

Boldface words appear in the glossary.

Be a Good Sport

We all like to win! But being a good sport can be more important than winning. Good sportsmanship is not only about sports. Any time we work or play with others, we should show respect and fairness. Good sports are always winners!

Stop and Listen

The baseball game was about to begin. The **coach** called the team together. He told them how he wanted them to play. He gave them important tips. They listened closely. A good sport always listens to others.

Win Well

Nate played a game of **chess** with his sister. Nate won the game. His sister was upset. Nate told her that she had played well. He did not make fun of her for losing. A good sport wins with **grace**.

9

Losing Is OK

James and Zion played in a big soccer game. Their team lost by one point. The boys were **disappointed**. But after the game, they talked about how they could play better next time. They didn't feel bad anymore. Good sports learn from losing.

Be a Team Player

Robert worked with a group in **science** class. Each person in his group had a job. Robert did his part. He also helped the others. Everyone worked together. A good sport does their share of the work.

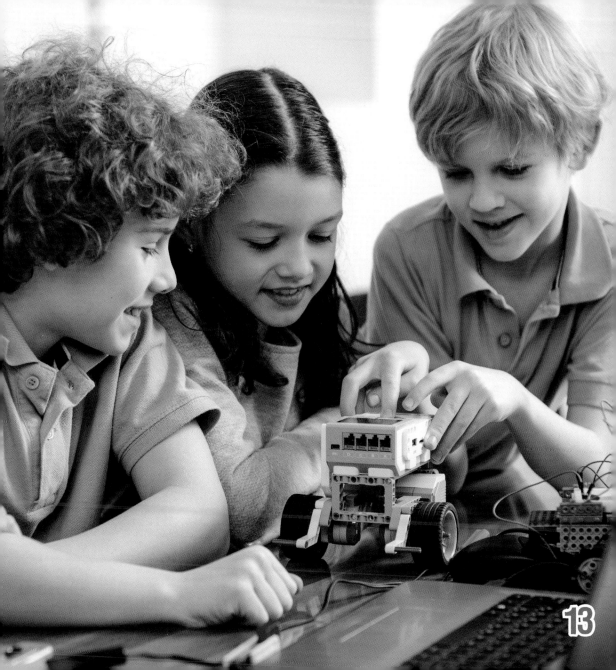
13

Lend a Hand

Brandon was running a race in gym class. The boy running next to him tripped and fell to the ground. Brandon stopped running and held out his hand to help the other boy up. A good sport helps others.

15

Do Your Part

Charlie was going to play ball with his friends. His family was helping with the neighborhood yard sale. Charlie's mom asked him to stay and help. Charlie said okay. He would play ball later. A good sport helps out and does not **complain**.

High Five!

Shaina's team lost their soccer game. They were sad, but they gave high fives to the players on the other team. They said, "Good game!" Win or lose, good sports shake hands or give a high five after a game.

Support the Team

Tim hurt his foot at baseball practice. He could not play in the game the next day. Tim still showed up to the game. He **cheered** for his team. A good sport **supports** his team even if he can't play.

GLOSSARY

cheer: to shout encouragement, or words that make someone or a group feel more assured and hopeful

chess: a game for two players in which 16 pieces are moved around a checkered board according to a set of rules

coach: someone who trains and teaches someone or a team in a sport or activity

complain: to say or write about being unhappy

disappointed: feeling let down or unhappy

grace: a kind and polite way of acting

science: the study of the way things work and the way things are in the world around you

support: to hold up and help

FOR MORE INFORMATION

BOOKS

Graves, Sue. *I Want to Win*. Minneapolis, MN: Free Spirit Publishing, 2017.

Smith, Bryan. *If Winning Isn't Everything, Why Do I Hate to Lose?* Boys Town, NE: Boys Town Press, 2015.

WEBSITES

How To Be A Good Sport

fugazi.kidshealth.org/en/kids/good-sport.html?WT.ac=p-ra
Check out tips for handling losing and being a good sport.

Practice Being a Good Sport

www.pbs.org/parents/crafts-and-experiments/practice-being-a-good-sport
Find a fun activity you can do with your parents to learn the value of sportsmanship.

INDEX